God Made Me Awesome!

FUN ACTIVITIES & DEVOTIONS FOR GIRLS

BroadStreet KIDS

BroadStreet Kids
Savage, Minnesota, USA

BroadStreet Kids is an imprint of BroadStreet Publishing Group, LLC.
Broadstreetpublishing.com

God Made Me Awesome!

© 2018 by BroadStreet Publishing®

978-1-4245-5691-5

Devotional entries written by Carol Garborg.
Activities created by Michelle Winger.

Cover and interior design by Chris Garborg | garborgdesign.com
Compiled and edited by Michelle Winger | literallyprecise.com

Printed in the United States of America.

18   19   20   21   22   23   24   7   6   5   4   3   2   1

Be Still

Be still and know that I am God.
I will be praised in all the nations;
I will be praised throughout the earth.
PSALM 46:10 NCV

Jessica could never sit still. She couldn't watch TV without wiggling her foot. She couldn't sit in class without bouncing her leg up and down. Her hands were always fidgeting or texting or twirling her hair. Being still was out of the question. She loved to be moving and doing.

Sometimes that's how we are on the inside. We can't "sit still" inside because we're busy thinking and stressing out...

- about a stupid comment we made yesterday
- about how to fix a broken friendship
- about falling apart at dance tryouts

Instead of stressing out, talk to God. Then just chill and be still, knowing that he is God.

God, sometimes I get worked up on the inside
and get really stressed out. Remind me to quiet my heart
and remember that you are a big, powerful God.

Change one letter
to create new words and
turn MESS into REST!

MESS

_ _ _ _   Don't hit

_ _ _ _   Light sprinkle

_ _ _ _   Things to do written on paper

_ _ _ _   Can't find

_ _ _ _   Update status

_ _ _ _   Annoying animal

REST

Do and Don't

*Don't worry about anything; instead, pray about everything.
Tell God what you need, and thank him for all he has done.*
PHILIPPIANS 4:6 NLT

Problems are like magnets. They attract all your attention. You think about them, talk about them, text about them, and journal about them. And the number one thing people do is worry about problems. All. The. Time.

Don'ts can be discouraging because they tell you what you *can't* do.

- Don't forget to wash your hands.
- Don't go outside until you finish your homework.
- Don't worry.

Do's are empowering because they tell you how you *can* change the situation. In this verse, you find out what you can do to change the situation you're in.

- Pray about everything.
- Tell God what you need.
- Thank him, even though you haven't seen an answer yet. It's coming!

What would help you remember to pray and tell God about everything instead of worrying so much?

*God, my mind gets stuck on problems like bees buzz around honey.
Help me to focus on you instead of on my problems.
When I'm tempted to worry, would you remind me to thank you
that you've got things covered?*

Cross out every second letter, then write the remaining letters on the spaces below to reveal the hidden message.

DNORNFOLTOWFOLRERNY

GENMISHGTIYENRANTEUROLBCAA

CPERHATYNAKBPOVUWT

GENBIEHITAYSRPETVNEL

__ __ _____ _____ ____ ____ ____

_____.

_____.

Messing Up

To him who is able to keep you from stumbling and to present you before his glorious presence without fault and with great joy.
JUDE 24 NIV

Zoe and her dad were hiking down a steep road, carefully placing one foot in front of the other. Zoe's left foot hit loose gravel on the rocky road and she stumbled, tripped, and fell onto her back. Zoe's dad held out his hand and helped pull her up. She came away with a few bruises and a little embarrassment.

When the Bible talks about stumbling, it's talking about making mistakes and messing up. A thoughtless word. An angry look. The results can be a lot more serious than bruises and embarrassment. A quick, unkind word can ruin a friendship. An angry look can hurt feelings. When it's past, we feel terrible. We really do. But the damage sometimes has already been done.

The Lord is your helper. He can keep you from slipping, stumbling, and messing up. He can keep you from making mistakes you really don't mean, or want, to make and keep you standing. His specialty is taking failure and turning it into success.

*Dear God, thanks for your patience with me.
Thanks for continuing to work in my life even when I mess up.
I want to let you have your way in me.*

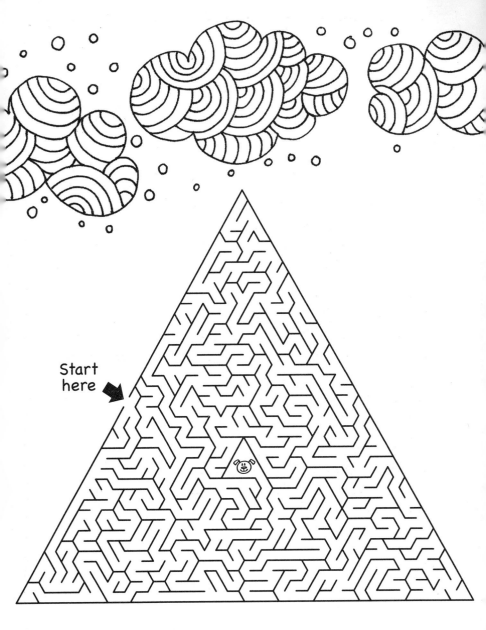

Start
here

Help Zoe find her puppy.

Designer Label

*We are God's masterpiece. He has created us anew in Christ Jesus,
so we can do the good things he planned for us long ago.*
EPHESIANS 2:10 NLT

You can tell a real Coach purse from a knock-off by the label. That label tells you who made the purse—and that's where the real value is. Who made the purse makes all the difference. It tells you about the quality, the detail, and ultimately how much the purse is worth.

You were made by the Creator of heaven and earth. You're his masterpiece and you wear his label. That's where your value comes from. It doesn't come from what you have, do, or what people say about you any more than pasting a "Coach" label on a cheap purse turns it into the real thing.

Your value won't change—because who made you doesn't change. If things get tough or someone questions your value by calling you names, remember who made you. Remember your value.

*Dear God, I am your masterpiece: a priceless person in
your eyes. Thank you for making me who I am. Not someone else.
Not different. Just me.*

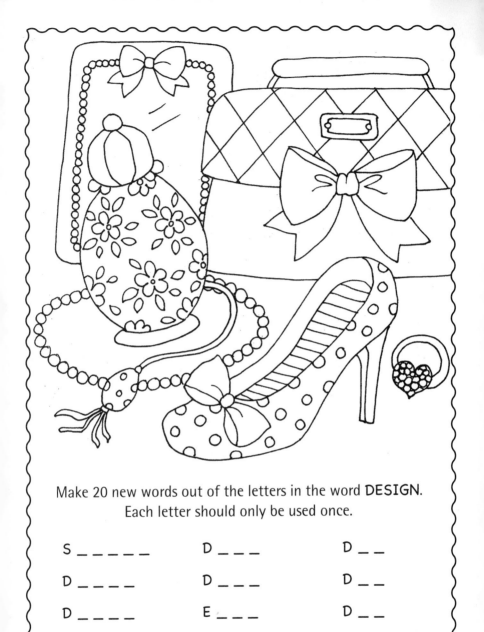

Make 20 new words out of the letters in the word **DESIGN**.
Each letter should only be used once.

S _ _ _ _ _

D _ _ _ _

D _ _ _ _

S _ _ _ _

D _ _ _

D _ _ _

D _ _ _

D _ _ _

D _ _ _

E _ _ _

S _ _ _

S _ _ _

S _ _ _

S _ _ _

D _ _

D _ _

D _ _

D _ _

E _ _

S _ _

Circle the 10 differences between
these 2 pictures, and then color!

Beach Sand

God, your thoughts are precious to me. They are so many! If I could count them, they would be more than all the grains of sand.
PSALM 139:17-18 NCV

A day at the beach means a day of sun, water, and lots of sand. Sand sprinkled on your beach towel, sand squishing underneath your toes, sand clinging to your swimsuit, and sand sticking to your fingers when you're trying to eat your picnic lunch. Tiny grains of sand everywhere!

If you scooped up a handful of sand and tried to count the tiny grains, could you do it? Impossible! And it's just as impossible to count all the thoughts—the good thoughts—that God has about you. If you could count them, they would be more than all the grains of sand on the seashore.

How do you picture God? What do you picture him thinking and saying about you? How does it line up with this verse?

Dear God, whenever I start to question who I am and what you think of me, help me to stop, remember, and thank you that your thoughts are more than the sands on the seashore.

Choose a word for each part of speech specified.
Then use your words to fill in the story below.

1._____ adjective

2._____ name

3._____ adjective

4._____ verb (past tense)

5._____ noun

6._____ verb (past tense)

7._____ verb (past tense)

8._____ verb (past tense)

9._____ verb (+ING)

10._____ name

11._____ verb (past tense)

12._____ adjective

13._____ adjective

14._____ adjective

15._____ animal

16._____ name

17._____ verb (past tense)

18._____ place

19._____ food

20._____ noun (plural)

21._____ verb (past tense)

22._____ adjective

At the Beach

It was a hot __1__ day. __2__ decided it would be a __3__ day for
the beach, so we __4__ into the __5__ and drove to the ocean.
The sand __6__, the water __7__, and the sun __8__.

"Let's go __9__!" I said to __10__, and we __11__ into the __12__ water.

We played in the __13__ waves until we were __14__.

"Look! I see a __15__ in the water!" shouted __16__.

Everyone __17__ and swam back to the shore.

"Well, we better go back to the __18__ now," I said.
"Mom has probably made __19__ for us all."

We packed up our __20__ and __21__ home.

That was one of the __22__ days all summer.

Choosing Friends

*The righteous choose their friends carefully,
but the way of the wicked leads them astray.*
PROVERBS 12:26 NIV

Hmm, what should I wear? thought Harper as she stood in her closet. *Will it be the pink tunic with black leggings or the three-quarter sleeve tee with skinny jeans?* Big decision. Choosing friends is a little like choosing clothes, only far more important of course. Actually being *careful* about picking friends isn't something we usually think about. After all, some friendships just happen.

Here are some questions to think about:

- Where are my friends headed? (And we're not talking about the mall here.) If I lived like they're living, how would I end up?

- What's important to my friends? Is it what I want to be important to me?

- What kinds of things do they encourage me to do?

- Do they make what's right easy or hard?

- Do my closest friends share my faith in Jesus?

The answers will empower you to decide if they're the best friends to have or if they're headed in a direction you'd rather not be going.

God, thank you for good friends. I don't know what I'd do without them. Help me to be careful choosing my friends.

Hope

Those who hope in the L̲̲ᴏ̲ʀᴅ will renew their strength.
They will soar on wings like eagles;
they will run and not grow weary,
they will walk and not be faint.
ɪsᴀɪᴀʜ 40:31 ɴɪᴠ

Hope is that sparkle of excitement inside that keeps us going. There's always that possibility that even if today isn't that fun or exciting, something better will come along. What happens when what you hope for doesn't happen? Then what?

Everyone talks about hoping *for something*—a good grade or a spot on the softball team. The problem is that people and circumstances change. If that's where our hope is, we'll be disappointed—a lot.

Read the three words after "hope" in the verse above. It says to be hopeful *in someone.* God never changes. He's always good, always loving, always in control. Even when it doesn't seem like it. Even when bad things happen. Hope in God is never disappointed.

Dear God, I know that you've put desires in my heart, to do, go, and be different things. But things and people and places change. Help me to put my hope in you—the only thing that stays the same from day to day.

```
                  R W R
                  H S O B W
                  C C R V H
          L V     Q Q G O N     T A
      Q Z K P     E P P     P P Z P
      L Y D M X E E V E I L E B
      Y T U A E B R E F R E S H
        P Q N   P V U     H F P
                D N R Q D
        D E V E L O P C N Y H
        F W P S   U     E G E Q
        Z I P G   Z     P B I Y
          F G     Q     Q W
                  S
                  E
                  U
                  Q
                  I
                  N
                  U
                  M
      A E P A T I E N C E E F Z
        M O A Y E X T N M O B
        F L O E E N I H S M S
        M O S S O L B R B A V
        F R A G R A N C E T H
        H Q S D O Y P H Q U S
          T R C M O O L B R
          F R E W O L F L E
```

Find these words

BEAUTY	ENDURE	MATURE
BELIEVE	FLOWER	PATIENCE
BLOOM	FRAGRANCE	REFRESH
BLOSSOM	GROW	SHINE
DEVELOP	HOPE	UNIQUE

The Hidden You

LORD, *You have searched me and known me.*
You know when I sit down and when I stand up;
You understand my thoughts from far away.
PSALM 139:1-2 HCSB

She had two strikes against her. First, she was a woman in a country where women weren't important. Second, she was a bad woman. She had done so many bad things no one wanted to be her friend, which is why she grabbed her bucket and walked past the chickens and sheep to get water at the village well—all alone.

Truth was, even though she seemed strong on the outside, she hurt on the inside. Because it hurts not to have people like you. But she brushed away that thought as she brushed the sweat from her forehead. *Boy, it is hot out here!*

At the well she met a man unlike any other person. His name was Jesus.

Jesus talked to her.

Jesus was kind to her.

Jesus knew all about her. He told her that he wanted to give her a gift, a gift of living water and of eternal life.

Just like Jesus knew that woman, he knows you. Even when you've done something bad, Jesus loves you. He knows all about you and he wants to give you the same gift he gave her—kindness, hope, and eternal life.

Dear Jesus, you're not like anyone who ever lived. You're God! You know everything about me and you came so that I would have life.

Find the
hidden you.

Start here

It All Counts

Whatever you do, whether in word or deed, do it all in the name of the Lord Jesus, giving thanks to God the Father through him.
COLOSSIANS 3:17 NIV

If you divided this list into two different sets, what would they be?

Apples, oranges, carrots, squash, pineapple, green beans, strawberries. Easy, right?

How about this list? *Reading your Bible, playing Uno with your cousin, going to youth group, praying, going to the zoo*

Most people, and you may or may not be one of them, put them into two categories: things that are spiritual and things that are not. Things that you do for God and things that you do just because.

The truth is, *anything* you do can be a beautiful act of worship to God. Unloading the dishwasher, vacuuming the living room, even picking up dog poop (well, maybe not). You can practice piano as if Jesus were sitting in the room, do your English assignment as if he were going to read it the next day. Not out of a sense of fear, like, *I have to get this perfect or God will be disappointed*—but out of joy, like, *I love the Lord and want to give him my best.*

What's something you never thought of before as something you could do to show your love to God? Would you change anything about how you did it?

Dear God, I want everything I do to show my love for you—because you deserve the best. Thank you that even the ordinary things in my day can praise you.

Use the doodles on
this page to create
your own pictures.

Dot Square Game—Play with a friend!

Connect two flowers with a line. Take turns connecting flowers.
If you draw a line that completes a box, put your initials in that box—
it's yours! Whenever a player makes a box, they get to take another
turn. At the end of the game, count the boxes with your initials in it.
The player with the most boxes wins!

The Munchies

You satisfy me more than the richest feast
I will praise you with songs of joy.
PSALM 63:5 NLT

Cheesy pizza. Walking tacos. Juicy steaks with mashed potatoes.
Stir fry with noodles or a huge taco salad. If you've got a case of
the munchies, what would you want to eat? Whether it's an all-
you-can-eat buffet or hamburger and potato salad feast, munchies
are a part of every sleepover, youth retreat, and birthday party.
Salty, sour, gooey, sweet they tease your tongue in a way that begs
for more.

Knowing God, who he is and what he likes, satisfies more than the
biggest and best feast. Not in a "my-stomach-is-full" kind of way
but in a "you-put-a-smile-on-my-face" way. Like the way you feel
after you've had your favorite meal, kind of happy and content.
Out of that happiness bubbles up songs of joy.

How is it that God satisfies you?

Dear God, people say that spending time with you satisfies
in a way that nothing else can. I want to experience that.
To slow down, really listen, and get to know you
the same way you know me.

Circle the two pictures that are exactly the same.

Raging Ocean

If any of you needs wisdom, you should ask God for it.
He is generous to everyone....But when you ask God, you must
believe and not doubt. Anyone who doubts is like a wave
in the sea, blown up and down by the wind.

JAMES 1:5-6 NCV

Should I, or shouldn't I?

What if I don't? What if I do?

How will it work out? What if it doesn't work out?

What do I do?!

If you've got a choice to make, some of these thoughts might be tearing around inside your brain, threatening to make your head explode. Who do you ask over for a birthday party, what do you say to the boy you really like, or should you try out for the volleyball team? Whether it seems like a big decision to anyone else, to *you* it really is a big deal. So what do you do?

First, just ask God for wisdom. Then, *believe* that he'll answer. God is generous with his wisdom! So ask boldly, knowing he'll answer.

Then decide. Go ahead, choose. Don't second guess yourself. Don't doubt. Don't wonder, *Did I do the right thing?* Just do it. When you doubt or are indecisive, you're like a wave on the sea that's blown around, back and forth. It's not doing anything or going anywhere.

Dear God, I haven't always thought of you as generous. I'm sorry.
Please give me wisdom for the choice I need to make.
Thank you that you will.

Create your own picture using the sketch starter below

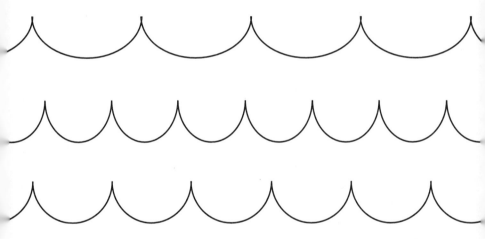

Caved In

*Truthful lips endure forever,
but a lying tongue, only a moment.*
PROVERBS 12:19 HCSB

"Now what are we going to do?" Daniella asked. Ahead of their car the road was caved in.

"It has to be from all the rain we've gotten," her dad commented. "It's eroded the foundation of dirt from under the road. Looks like we'll have to back up and go the other way around."

Daniella groaned. She wanted in the worst way to see Mount Rushmore. But it didn't look like that wasn't going to happen any time soon. Her vacation was a total washout.

Caved in and washed out is what happens when we don't tell the truth. Speaking what's true is like building a road on a foundation of rock. Rain can pour down and that road won't be washed out. Lying is like building a road on sand. Rain pours down and the road washes out. The road doesn't last and neither does a lie. Someone will always find out the truth. Someone who does what Jesus says and tells the truth is like the house that lasts. The truth lasts forever.

Whether you tell just a little bit of untruth or a full-blown lie, a lying tongue will always be found out. Truthful lips last forever.

*Dear God, if I'm ever tempted to lie, help me remember
that in the end the truth is what is going to last.
Keep me from everything untrue.*

Start
here

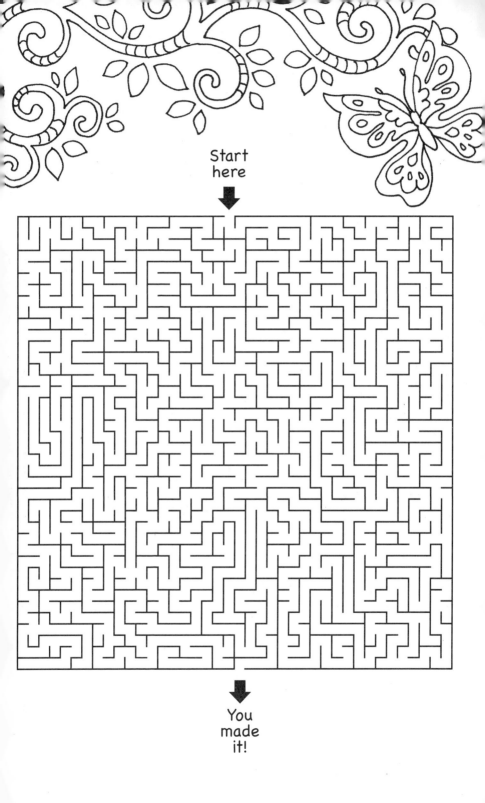

You
made
it!

Beauty that Lasts

Beauty does not last;
but a woman who fears the LORD
will be greatly praised.
PROVERBS 31:30 NLT

"I cannot believe I have to wear my sister Jenae's hand-me-downs," Valeria moaned. "They're two years old! Everyone knows those old jeans and tops are *so* out of style!"

Whether you're talking about smartphone versions or the latest fashion, neither of them last. Beauty isn't much different. God makes each of us beautiful—in a way that lasts.

Sure you might have a beautiful smile or deep brown eyes or a cute dimple in your cheek. That kind of beauty, while it's definitely nice to have, will someday fade. What doesn't fade is a woman—that would be you!—who fears, or respects, God. That's a different kind of beauty that lasts on and on.

Dear God, thank you for the different ways beauty shows up
in different people around me—in deep brown eyes and long
eyelashes and curly hair and straight hair. Thank you too for
those people who are an example of beauty that lasts.
That's the kind of beauty I want to have!

Use your creativity to make this girl beautiful on the outside.

Write down some characteristics that make us beautiful on the inside.

Shine!

"Let your light shine before others, that they may see your good deeds and glorify your Father in heaven."
MATTHEW 5:16 NIV

It's a Friday night and you're at a friend's house for a movie and sleepover. The electricity goes out and everyone giggles and screams because it's both scary and fun. But after a few minutes of sitting in total darkness, it starts to get eerie and you're like "Someone get a flashlight, a candle, anything!"

When you help your mom make the beds, or write your grandma a thank-you note, or offer to play with the little neighborhood kids so their mom can have a break, or you tell someone about Jesus, you're like a flashlight. You're being a light that shines into the darkness and shows other people who God is. The point of doing good deeds isn't to show people how wonderful you are; it's to show others what God is like and who he is. It's pointing them to him.

What are some good deeds that would show someone what God is like?

Dear God, thank you that I can praise you by doing good things. Thank you that I can show your light by doing what is good. Please give me creative ideas on how to do good for others.

Figure out the secret message by using the code below.

◎	▲	☼	□	●	✓	❖	◆	❀	✚	☺	✐	∿
A	B	C	D	E	F	G	H	I	J	K	L	M

★	↑	↓	●	⌘	❀	✕	⁂	▣	✺	✄	※	❄
N	O	P	Q	R	S	T	U	V	W	X	Y	Z

YOU ARE A

BRIGHT SHINING

LIGHT FOR JESUS!

Anywhere, Everywhere

I can never escape from your Spirit! I can never get away from your presence! If I ride the wings of the morning, if I dwell by the farthest oceans, even there your hand will guide me, and your strength will support me.
PSALM 139:7, 9-10 NLT

Mariana flopped into the hammock and began to swing. Back here in the yard, behind the tool shed, next to the daisies, under the oak tree was her favorite spot to get away and talk to God.

When it comes to spending time with God (some people call it doing devotions, but it's really just meeting up with God), there's nowhere we can go where he is not. Everywhere we go, God will be there with us.

You can meet God—going on a bike ride early in the morning, climbing a tree and telling him about your day, pulling the covers over your head late at night and using a flashlight to read your Bible, going for a run around the school track, praying for your family while you're on the treadmill, or swinging in a hammock and praising him for all the amazing creation you see.

Where and how do you enjoy meeting with God? How creative can you get?

Dear God, you are everywhere and that's amazing! If I can spend time with my friends at the mall, in my living room, or at a park, I can do the same with you. You are my friend.

You
made
it!

Start
here

Dot Square Game—Play with a friend!

Connect two flowers with a line. Take turns connecting flowers.
If you draw a line that completes a box, put your initials in that box—
it's yours! Whenever a player makes a box, they get to take another
turn. At the end of the game, count the boxes with your initials in it.
The player with the most boxes wins!

That Hurts!

God is the Father who is full of mercy and all comfort.
He comforts us every time we have trouble, so when others have
trouble, we can comfort them with the same comfort God gives us.
2 CORINTHIANS 1:3-4 NCV

"Ow, that hurts!"

Whether it's a stubbed toe, a sprained wrist, or a broken ankle,
your body has a tremendous capacity—to hurt! Some hurts go
deeper than others. They're the ones inside that no one sees. Hurt
feelings from someone's careless or angry words. Embarrassment
from a mistake you made. Shame from what someone did to you,
something that's not your fault. Confusion about a divorce. Hurts
like those can seem almost too big for words.

With God, you don't have to say anything; he just understands. He
is full of mercy and full of comfort. Just being near him can take
some of the hurt away. He also comforts by using others who have
been through the same thing. Talk to them and ask, "How did God
comfort you when you were hurting?"

Dear God, I hurt. Sometimes I hurt so much it's hard to talk.
You see inside me. Wrap your arms around me.
I need to know you're near.

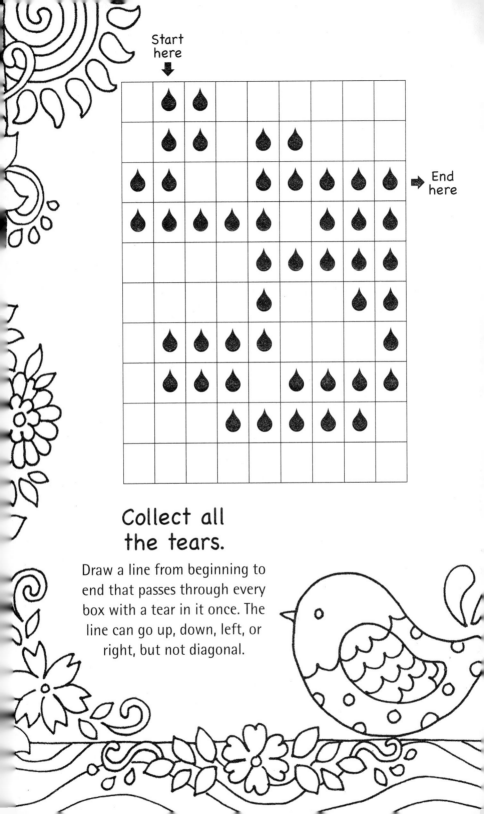

Start
here

End
here

Collect all the tears.

Draw a line from beginning to end that passes through every box with a tear in it once. The line can go up, down, left, or right, but not diagonal.

Feeling the Way I Do

When I am afraid,
I put my trust in you.
PSALM 56:3 NIV

"Come on now. Don't be afraid. It's not that bad. In fact, it'll be fun."

"But, Dad," said Alex, looking down at the zipline's forty-foot drop, "I *am* afraid."

People mean well. They really do. But when they say things like "don't be afraid" or "don't be down" or "don't be discouraged," it's like telling us to stop feeling the way we do. The problem is, we *are* down, we *are* afraid, or we might be feeling very discouraged.

God gets this, which is why the psalms are packed with emotions like fear, frustration, and anger. The psalmist doesn't hide his feelings from God; he tells it like it is.

Feeling fear isn't abnormal or something to be ashamed of. So instead of stuffing fear feelings into a corner of your heart or trying to ignore them, go to God when you are afraid. Even if someone has told you not to be afraid. Even if it's something you don't think you should be afraid of. God won't dismiss you and say, "Well, just get over it." Instead he says, "Trust in me."

Dear God, I'm afraid. I'm afraid to _____ (fill in the blank).
But I put my trust in you.

Write every third letter on the spaces below
to reveal the secret message.

Start
here

B W I E I W
T A
I L
T I
S F
D L
O L
U R
N T
R L
A A
L R
T N
I
U

_____ _____ _____ _____ _____ _ _.

_ _____ _____.

Me First?

Be devoted to one another in love.
Honor one another above yourselves.
ROMANS 12:10 NIV

Adalyn looked down at the plate of lasagna between her and her sister. She was hungry for seconds. Two hours of soccer practice would do that to you. But there was only one small piece of lasagna left, and her sister wanted it too. What should she do?

A woman in the Bible faced a similar dilemma. When she was down to her last meal, the prophet Elijah asked her for something to eat. If she gave it to Elijah, she would go hungry. If she kept it for herself, he would go hungry. What was she going to do?

We're all pretty good at looking out for ourselves. After all, if we don't who will, right? Yet if we're followers of Jesus, standing up for others instead of ourselves is the way to go. The woman in the Bible did what Elijah asked and gave him the meal. God rewarded her big time. For the next few years, she never ran out of food. That's how it is when we do what God asks. We take care of trusting and obeying, and he takes care of the rest.

Dear God, help me to trust that when you ask me
to put others first, you will provide for me.

Find these words

Word search grid:

```
      Q L T J                   U O J A
    I E H O I A               J A M M X E
  C Q O D R H U N           F A Q K T D Y R
Q G N W L V A N R B     O A Y L Z T E W O K
U O X T H G I L E D R B A D Q D Y V L V N
R U X G Y H D Y I G K P E M O M N O Y A T
U W Q O O T X C I Q G E V O L R R T S F W
R E G A R D C V L I Q K Y O Y Z E I I X O
C W F F T R E A S U R E H O S V P O N F U
  W A M D F I Y E W U V O H J S Z N T T
  V B T E O G I T S T O X Z M E S M O E
    Z C C E V O A W Q R X E Q L V H A
    H C H T T Z I N B P C H E R I S H
      V L R B S C V R P V L B Z E S
        Y Y E T E K Y A Q Y C R S
          P Z S R T Q C H C I C
          J M P Q P X F M A
            Z P E C C D M
            A D C A H
            U H T
            N
```

Find these words

ADMIRE	DELIGHT	HONOR
ADORE	DEVOTION	LOVE
APPRECIATE	ESTEEM	REGARD
APPROVE	FAVOR	RESPECT
CHERISH	FORGIVE	TREASURE

Saying Thank You

I thank my God every time I remember you.
PHILIPPIANS 1:3 NIV

Saying thank you can be fun! Whether someone gave you a birthday gift, did you a favor, or just came to mind because you think they're great, you have so many things to say thank you for. God puts people in your life who make you feel great. Telling them you appreciate them can make them feel great too.

Who are three people you're especially thankful for? List something specific they've done that you're thankful for.

Choose one of the creative ways below to thank each of them. Or, come up with your own creative thank you!

- Take a selfie of you smiling and send it to that person along with, "You put a smile on my face today. Thank you!"

- Take a video of yourself singing, "Thank-you, thank-you" to the tune of Happy Birthday. Send it to that person.

- Tell someone what that person did for you. Good news travels quickly and you can be sure the person will hear about it.

Dear God, thank you for amazing people who fill my life with good things. I'm so happy they're in my life. Show me the best way to thank them for what they do.

Use the letters in the
word **THANKS** to
create new words.

H _ _ _ _   T _ _ _
S _ _ _ _   T _ _ _
S _ _ _ _   T _ _ _
T _ _ _ _   A _ _
T _ _ _ _   A _ _
A _ _ _   A _ _
H _ _ _   H _ _
H _ _ _   H _ _
H _ _ _   S _ _
S _ _ _   T _ _
S _ _ _
T _ _ _

Knock, Knock

"Everyone who asks will receive. The one who searches will find. And everyone who knocks will have the door opened."

LUKE 11:10 NCV

Knock, knock

Who's there?

Cow says.

Cow says who?

No, silly, cow says moo!

A knock-knock joke wasn't exactly what Jesus had in mind when he told his disciples the verse above. (But hey, he probably would have liked it.) What Jesus was really saying is when you knock on a door, you expect the door to open. In the same way, when you pray you can expect God to answer.

First he says...

Ask: Come right out and ask God for what you need.

Seek: That just means be on the lookout for God's answer. Pay attention to anything he might be telling you.

Knock: Be persistent. Don't give up if the answer doesn't come right away

Be encouraged. God does answer prayer!

Dear God, you love to answer prayer! Thank you for that. Help me to keep hoping for the answer to my prayers and not give up.

Start here to find Fluffy.

Muddy Latte

*Religion that God our Father accepts as pure and faultless is...
to keep oneself from being polluted by the world.*
JAMES 1:27 NIV

What's your favorite thing to drink? Sweet tea? An icy Coke? What about a thick strawberry banana smoothie? Or perhaps you're more of a latte person.

Imagine you've got two glasses, one with latte and the other with muddy water. You pour a little latte into a third glass along with a little muddy water. (After all, they do kind of look the same, right?) Stir them together. How do you think it would taste? Probably like a whole lot of yuck.

When you follow God, you can't do what God wants most of the time and what you want a little of the time. You can't do a little of what he says and mix in a little of what the world says—like encourage your friend Melody, and then make fun of Krista. Or give money to a mission project, then refuse to give your little brother a piece of gum. Doing that is like polluting latte with muddy water.

God loves all of you. Love him with all your heart, all your mind, and everything you've got.

*Dear God, I want all in. I want all of me to be yours,
every area of my life—my studies, my relationship with others.
Be the Lord of my life.*

Circle the two pictures that are exactly the same.

Dot Square Game—Play with a friend!

Connect two flowers with a line. Take turns connecting flowers.
If you draw a line that completes a box, put your initials in that box—
it's yours! Whenever a player makes a box, they get to take another
turn. At the end of the game, count the boxes with your initials in it.
The player with the most boxes wins!

Homemade Ice Cream

There is a time for everything,
and a season for every activity under the heavens.
He has made everything beautiful in its time.
ECCLESIASTES 3:1, 11 NIV

Summers are made up of swimming, vacations, camps, sleepovers, sleeping in, and of course, ice cream. Double scoops of chocolate chip heaped high in a waffle cone or cake batter flavor in a dish drizzled with chocolate and crushed Oreos. Yum!

All the deliciousness of ice cream comes when milk, cream, sugar and a bunch of other goodies are poured into an ice cream machine where it's churned and turned until it's frozen and creamy. Twenty minutes later, you can plunge your spoon into thick, icy creaminess. Take the mixture out any sooner, though, and all you'll have is a soupy mess. If you want ice cream, you've got to wait.

Some of the best things in life are worth waiting for.

Dear God, your plans are perfect. Your plans are good.
I want to follow your plan to keep myself pure,
both with what I think and what I do.

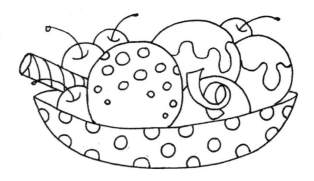

```
                I  F  Q  U  D
             N  C  V  Y  X  K  O
             Y  E  Q  L  I  E  I
             A  C  J  U  D  V  U
             B  R  X  B  F  E  M
             E  T  Q  M  R
          G  Z  A  D  I  V  Y  U  K
       X  B  U  M  U  C  F  T  U  J  G
    G  N  I  P  M  A  C  U  H  O  B  F  D
    N  S  R  A  C  T  I  V  I  T  Y  D  R
    D  B  H  S  X  G  V  Y  N  F  L  L  U
    B  O  E  L  S  Y  A  X  G  M  X  F  A
    R  S  G  A  X  U  B  J  X  Y  V  N  K
       F  E  S  U  D  N  L  F  U  H  Z
       C  S  G  T  O  S  A  M  Y
    S  A  U  Q  R  E  I  G  T  M  X  C  F
 S  O  X  S  G  E  Z  T  F  X  Y  V  G  T  K
 U  N  E  U  Z  V  E  A  D  U  U  W  M  E  S
Z O  L  O  L  J  O  R  C  D  M  L  U  D  C  W  R
E I  V  A  S  L  P  W  A  F  R  O  Z  E  N  I  W
N C  H  A  M  A  E  W  V  N  T  V  F  V  Q  M  P
T I  M  E  N  B  E  N  V  R  E  D  T  Q  L  M  X
B L  W  Z  D  X  L  S  S  Z  V  W  R  T  T  I  O
X E  B  V  W  A  S  D  F  A  Y  Q  S  G  R  N  V
 D  C  Q  N  C  J  P  G  N  I  T  I  A  W  G
 S  W  E  E  T  I  A  X  V  U  C  S  L
```

Find these words

ACTIVITY

BEAUTIFUL

CAMPING

DELICIOUS

EVERYTHING

FROZEN

ICE CREAM

SEASON

SLEEPOVER

SWEET

SWIMMING

TIME

VACATION

WAITING

YUMMY

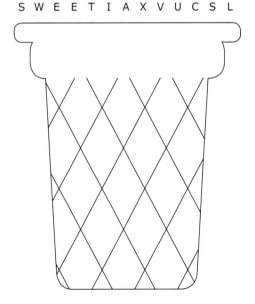

Deep Joy

In Your presence is fullness of joy;
In Your right hand there are pleasures forever.
PSALM 16:11 NASB

"What's the matter, Alessandra? You don't seem like yourself," Dad asked.

Alessandra *was* feeling down. She wasn't sure why. She just felt restless, almost like something was missing.

When something like joy is missing, it isn't like looking for a missing sock. You won't find it under the sofa cushion, behind the dresser, or stuck to your sheets. Joy comes from Someone—Jesus. Being with Jesus fills you with joy.

That's not to say, of course, that two scoops of ice cream on a summer day don't make you happy, or that water skiing with friends or screaming down the side of a roller coaster won't make you smile. But joy—deep down satisfaction—only comes from being with Jesus. It doesn't come from doing or having things, even though they might be fun. And it doesn't go away if something not-so-fun happens. The more time you read his Word and spend time with him, the more he'll fill you with joy!

Dear Jesus, you give me joy!
You satisfy like nothing else can. Thank you.

Change one letter at a time
to create new words and allow
God's **WORD** to give you **HOPE!**

WORD

_ _ _ _ _   Part of a hospital for specific patients

_ _ _ _ _   Bend out of shape

_ _ _ _ _   Stinging insect

_ _ _ _ _   Thin puff or streak

_ _ _ _ _   Speech impediment

_ _ _ _ _   Items written down

_ _ _ _ _   Cannot be found

_ _ _ _ _   Opposite of win

_ _ _ _ _   Fragrant flower

_ _ _ _ _   Get up

_ _ _ _ _   Ready to harvest

_ _ _ _ _   Thick string

HOPE

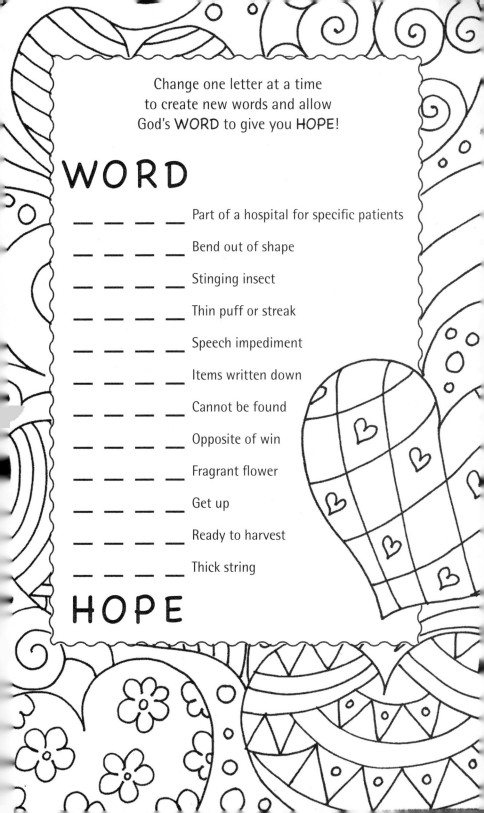

Sunshine in Rain

I trust him with all my heart.
He helps me, and my heart is filled with joy.
PSALM 28:7 NLT

It was Cassie's first time flying. She walked down the aisle of the plane and looked around until she found her seat in 16A, next to her dad, and right next to a window. She buckled her seatbelt and looked out the small window as buckets of rain poured down. Not a very sunshiny day. She hoped it would be sunshiny where she was going on vacation—to the beach.

The plane engine rumbled and soon they moved down the runway until up they soared through the rain and into the clouds. After ten minutes, Cassie was enjoying a cold Coke. She looked out the window and was surprised—above the clouds the sun shone bright and clear!

Sometimes the sun isn't missing; it's just tucked behind the cloud. Sometimes it seems like God is missing or he's so far away—when a pet dies, when we get left out, when our parents argue. But tucked behind everything, his presence is strong. Because he's there you can have joy knowing he's got this. No matter what happens— whether things turn out like you want them to or not—God is still good. God still loves you. That will *never* change.

Dear God, I trust you—when things are going well, when things are going not-so-well, when I'm confused, and when I don't understand. You are always there, and you are always good.

Word Search Puzzle

```
                        W V
                        H A
                        E W
    O Q                 R A                          M
     V L              K F M R Q G                  V R
      A X        Y H P I L M G I N V R          G C
       C N L Q I N D W M T W B T V E U      Y R
        A C B L H S S E N D O O G A T X D
       O W T E T C O U C O M R R X C F I
       S S G I H H R D N P R E S E N C E A
   J L U A V O Y K M R U W X O X V T Q I
    R Y Q N B Y N G T J E H P M B G Y W U T
    G J A E S H O W A C N P F F S Z I N X F
S O A R U M W I I H Z N F W W O D N I W T H K N H B L T
G E T U N C K J N B I A L K H L Q T Q S S O K O S H L U
    B E A C H K S N B M X B H O S W F X P G
    M O L S N M T P E E B C D Y Q U Q E X K
    R H D F D R L D Z U Z P Q Y U E R I T
     R F U M U X E Y R W N J D E O Y T M
     M A Q L I O C D X D O N W Q G X S
     M T I S V V L F E Y S S Y H U N C
    H B   A N F D Q C V K U T E L V   A E
   M X       Q H T N T E P A L N V      H R
   X A          N F D Q P T              C Z
    M              F O                    I J
                   S I
                   N L
                   U Y
```

Find these words

BEACH	HOPE	SUNSHINE
CHANGE	JOY	TRUST
CLOUDS	PRESENCE	VACATION
GOODNESS	RAIN	WARM
HELP	SOAR	WINDOW

Washing Machine

*Rest in God alone, my soul,
for my hope comes from Him.*
PSALM 62:5 HCSB

*Back and forth, around and around, right side up, and upside
down.* That's what happens to the clothes you throw in the washing
machine.

That's also what can happen to you, at least that's how life can
feel. Too many commitments, too many decisions, too many to-
do's, too many questions, and you just want to close your eyes and
yell, "Stop!"

When that happens, here are a few things that will help you keep sane:

- Go for a walk. Sometimes looking at a great big sky makes
  problems seem smaller and gives you focus.

- Listen to some worship music. Music can powerfully impact
  your spirit.

- Go for a run. Exercise increases endorphins that trigger
  positive feelings and give you more energy.

- Turn your attention to someone else who might be having an
  upside-down day.

- Go out for a latte and girl time with your mom or best friend.

Finally and most importantly, rest. Rest in God. Go to him and pray
about whatever is on your mind. Ask him to pull things together,
give you wisdom, and do what's best.

*Dear God, thanks for being my safe place, a place where I can rest.
I can go to you when my life seems upside down.*

Start here.

The Hand-Off

*Commit to the LORD whatever you do,
and he will establish your plans.*
PROVERBS 16:3 NIV

In the 2016 Summer Olympics, the United States' women's 4x100-meter relay track team dominated the sport and won the gold medal! In a relay race, four runners each take turns running as fast as they can. The first person carries the baton and sprints to the next runner on the team. Then she hands the baton off and the next runner takes it from there. Once she hands off the baton, it's not hers to worry about anymore.

Prayer works like that. Prayer is bringing our requests to God and then handing them off. He takes it from there, so we don't need to worry about it. We commit things to the Lord. (That just means take things to him and trust him.) That's our part. His part is "to establish our plans" or answer our prayers. The problem comes when we try to do both our part and his. Winning the race that way is impossible!

Why can it seem so hard to hand off our prayer requests to God?

Dear God, I realize that when I pray I don't always leave things in your hands. I take them back, like you can't be trusted. I'm sorry. Grow my faith.

Start
here
➡

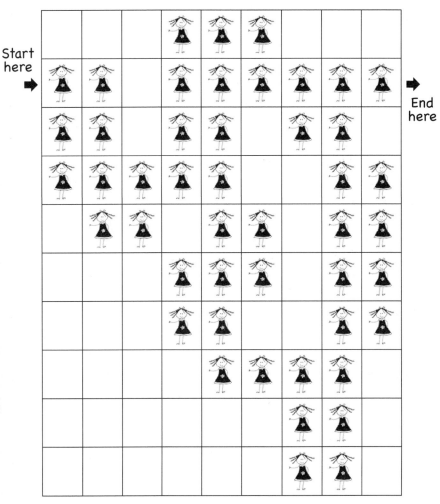

➡
End
here

Pass the baton to all the teammates in the grid.

Draw a line from beginning to end that passes through
every box with a person in it once.

The line can go up, down, left, or right, but not diagonal.

Growing

We ought always to thank God for you, brothers and sisters, and rightly so, because your faith is growing more and more, and the love all of you have for one another is increasing.

2 Thessalonians 1:3 niv

Spread out on the bed are magazines and books about horses. Posters of spotted Appaloosa horses, American Paints, and quarter horses cover the walls. Everywhere is horse heaven. This is the room of someone who loves horses. If you're into horses (or dogs, ballet, soccer, or anything really) you'll read, collect, research, and enjoy. The more you do, the more you'll learn because you can't help it. It's fun!

Faith in God is like that. The more you read God's Word and really dig in, the more time you spend with him, the more you thank him for what he's done, the more your faith with grow. And, the more you'll realize how great his love is for you.

What are some ways to do that? Sing a worship song while you're in the shower. Learn a verse from the Bible and tape it to the bathroom mirror. Read it out loud every time you see it. Whisper a just-between-you-and-me prayer when you wake up in the morning. Before closing your eyes at night tell God you love him, and then just be still and listen.

Dear God, I want my faith to grow, not to be small and weak but strong and deep. Keep showing me creative ways to grow in you.

Unscramble the words of some
different hobbies.

OOICLRGN _ _ _ _ _ _ _ _

RDIEGAN _ _ _ _ _ _ _

YHROHPTAOGP _ _ _ _ _ _ _ _ _ _

SAKRHBCOE GIRNDI _ _ _ _ _ _ _ _ _ _ _ _ _ _

CSOCRE _ _ _ _ _ _

LBLTEA _ _ _ _ _ _

GABYTISBTNI _ _ _ _ _ _ _ _ _ _

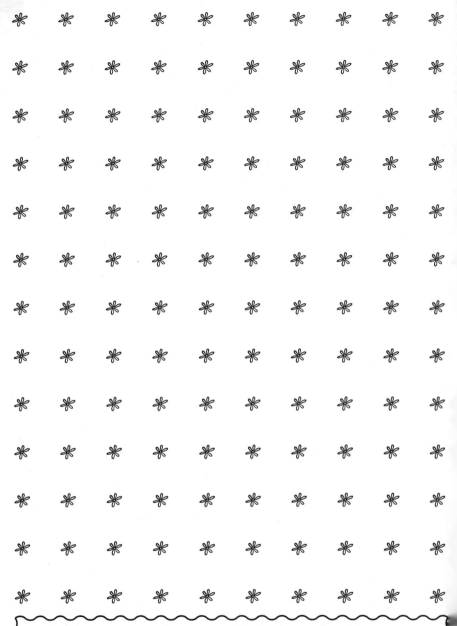

Dot Square Game—Play with a friend!

Connect two flowers with a line. Take turns connecting flowers.
If you draw a line that completes a box, put your initials in that box—
it's yours! Whenever a player makes a box, they get to take another
turn. At the end of the game, count the boxes with your initials in it.
The player with the most boxes wins!

Hello Summer

You set the boundaries of the earth,
and you made both summer and winter.
PSALM 74:17 NLT

When you rolled out of bed this morning, slipped on your clothes, and walked into the kitchen for breakfast, did you notice that... it's summer?! Summer sun and summer sunflowers. Beach time and sandcastles. Bonfires and picnics. Warm weather and juicy watermelon. God outdid himself when he created summer.

Here are some ideas to start off your summer:

- Have a summer-kickoff party in your neighborhood.

- Go gaga for games and invite friends to bring over a favorite game and favorite snack. Have a game marathon day and a different snack between each game.

- With your friends, make crafts as gifts and take them to people at a local nursing home.

- Create be-my-friend bracelets. Make two bracelets, one for you and another for one of the kids at your church. Tell them you'll pray for them every week.

Dear God, I love summer! Thank you for a break from school and time with friends and my family. Thanks for sunny skies and long days filled with all things summer.

```
                        G
                    A W W
                    D Q L S
                N B H C E A
                P J A G G G I
            A A P N A G H O L
            E X I P P O P Q C I
        C W M R V T F A W Y C N
        Y M A F Z A W N K R O Y G
      X I B P Y G O T B H A I S J R
      W S A J Y F B W K R T L J H Y O
    S F W L T S L L B Z Z P K E E S J E
    D G T R N H C I Y E E E I F U Y H Q D
  H R D A T E P A A G M A D R H R C C Y T A
  Q U P F T V F M S D Y X C B O M I F F S P N
S U N F L O W E R S S S S H H P Z P E I E S S O
D I M A K H Q K I M T U E M W V I A L N I H F J M
T Y M R U O N O L E M R E T A W J A K R N D P E T F E
Y R L N Z Z Y Q D U E R L T I Z S S N Z H E S L H P O L
C G L M K I I C H B F N Z W Y M L F C I J F U N C R D U Q U
                        I
                        H
                        S
N O D U K R N S O W X N Q S E L T S A C D N A S B Z Q Q K S
G E R I F N O B Q I U J R P C C Q R X Q T E Y R J V T W
U E H W S T Z M M D S V C T E E D V G G N H W T E O J R
S Z S K U R S U M F P N N D U P I C N I C F Y D I Y
U N K A S U M M E R A O L I C H P Q M P S S C P G N
P R G S I V D H G L L Q Q Z Z G S N A C K S J M
```

Find these words

BEACH	PICNIC	SUMMER
BONFIRE	SAILBOAT	SUNFLOWERS
FRIENDS	SAILING	SUNSHINE
LEMONADE	SANDCASTLES	SWIMMING
PARTY	SNACKS	WATERMELON

No Secrets

*O LORD, you have examined my heart and
know everything about me.*
PSALM 139:1 NLT

Sometimes reading the Bible seems more about someone else than
it does about us. Abraham and Sarah. Sampson and Delilah. *Their*
stories are in the Bible and God's whole story *is* the Bible. But
where do we fit in? What about what we're going through?

That's one reason Christians turn to the psalms. Psalms remind
us that God is a personal God. Musicians have put the psalms to
music, but the psalms are also great to use as prayers when we're
not really sure what to pray.

Try this way of praying and personalizing Psalm 139:

Lord, you know everything about me. You know when I go to
_____ (place) and when I do _____ (action
verb).

You understand when I'm thinking about _____
(circumstance or person) even when I lay down.

Before I'm tempted to talk about _____ (person, topic),
you know what I'm going to say.

When I think about your knowledge, it totally _____
(verb) me.

With you, Lord, there are no secrets!

*Dear Lord, you know me better than I know myself.
There's nothing you don't see and nothing you don't know.
I'm amazed and humbled all at once.*

Write every third letter on the spaces below
to reveal the secret message.

Start
here

GOD KNOWS EVERY

LITTLE THING

ABOUT ME!

The Top Three

What does the LORD require of you?
To act justly and to love mercy
and to walk humbly with your God.
MICAH 6:8 NIV

What are the top three girl names?

What are the top three music apps?

What are the top three selling snack crackers?

We all have our top three lists. Our top three favorite places to go on vacation. Our top three after school snacks. Our top three excuses for avoiding homework. You get the picture.

God has a top three too. Here are the top three things he's looking for in our lives.

- Act justly: Always do what's right and fair and just. Don't try to manipulate people and get your own way. Don't treat some people more importantly than others.

- Love mercy: Give people a break when they've messed up. Treat them with kindness even when they don't deserve it.

- Walk humbly: Instead of acting like you know it all and are better than everyone else, think of yourself—and others—like God does. He loves everyone just as much as the other.

Which of God's top three comes easiest for you? What's harder to do?

Dear God, teach me to act with justice,
to show people mercy, and to be humble.

Circle the 10 differences between these 2 pictures, and then color!

Great Wall

*A person without self-control is like
a city with broken-down walls.*
PROVERBS 25:28 NLT

The Great Wall of China is a wall of stone, earth, and bricks. It was built as a fortress to protect the country of China. In some places today the wall is over thirty feet high and over 5,000 miles, although it used to be much longer. Years ago if enemies wanted to attack China, they looked for a gap in the wall. They searched for weak points and made that their entry point.

When we don't have self-control, we're like a country or city that has broken-down walls. Self-control protects us by keeping us from impatience, anger, and doing things we regret. Without it, we open ourselves up to trouble and a lot of heartache. If someone loses their temper and yells at a friend, for instance, those words can never be taken back.

When you have self-control, you don't let what other people do or say about you control you. You control yourself. You don't need your mom to tell you not to have six pieces of pizza, because you control yourself—you know you'd get a stomachache. You don't need the teacher to tell you not to argue with your classmates, because you control yourself.

Protect your heart and do yourself a favor—practice self-control!

*Dear God, thank you for your Spirit who produces self-control
in me. Help me to listen to your Spirit and say yes to
self-control and no to anything else.*

Start here

You made it!

But, Why?

Do everything without complaining or arguing.
PHILIPPIANS 2:14 NCV

"But everyone has that brand of boots. Why can't I have them?"

"Church is the same every week, why do I have to go?"

"I hate creamy peanut butter. Why can't we ever buy chunky?"

Sound familiar? For forty years God heard similar things from the people of Israel. "Why did you have to bring us into the desert? We're so thirsty!" they complained. "Why can't we have bread?" they grumbled. "What's up with having no meat at all?" they muttered. Over and over God provided for all their needs but that didn't stop them from complaining.

We know we're not supposed to complain, but why not? What's the big deal? Psalm 78 says that complaining is basically telling someone, your parents for instance, "I don't trust you to take care of me. What you do for me isn't good enough" (verses 22-32). When you're thankful, you're saying, "Thanks for how you take care of me. I appreciate what you do."

That doesn't mean you can't ask for something. Just that when you ask, you don't dismiss the good your mom or dad has already done.

Dear God, help me show how much I appreciate all I have and the good my parent(s) do.

Figure out the secret message by using the code below.

◎	▲	☼	□	●	✓	❖	◆	❀	✝	☺	✏	♒
A	B	C	D	E	F	G	H	I	J	K	L	M

★	↑	↓	●	⌘	❀	✕	✳	▣	✹	✂	※	❄
N	O	P	Q	R	S	T	U	V	W	X	Y	Z

THEY WOULD PUT THEIR

TRUST IN GOD AND

WOULD NOT FORGET HIS

DEEDS BUT WOULD KEEP

HIS COMMANDS.

PSALM 78:7

_ _ _ _   _ _ _ _ _   _ _ _   _ _ _ _ _

_ _ _ _ _   _ _   _ _ _   _ _ _

_ _ _ _ _   _ _ _   _ _ _ _ _ _   _ _ _

_ _ _ _ _   _ _ _   _ _ _ _   _ _ _ _

_ _ _   _ _ _ _ _ _ _ _ _.

_ _ _ _ _ 78:7

Life Shared

Be happy with those who are happy, and weep with those who weep. Live in harmony with each other.
ROMANS 12:15 NLT

Life is so much better when it's shared.

Sharing life means...

- Sharing good news: "We're going hiking in Colorado for spring break! I can't wait!"

- Sharing something you just found out: "My new next-door neighbor has two bunnies. They're adorable."

- Sharing jokes and laughing together: "How many bananas can you eat if your stomach is empty? Only one. After that it's not empty anymore."

And it means...

- Sharing bad news, like your eleven-year-old dog Yolo just died.

- Throwing an arm around someone's shoulders when they're feeling down.

- Listening while your bestie tells you what is on her heart.

Sharing means togetherness. Sharing makes happy happier and sad a little more bearable. Who are your best sharing buddies? Why do you think friendship grows when you share?

Dear God, thank you for friends I can share with and friends who share with me. Life without them just wouldn't be the same. Help me to be the kind of person people have fun sharing life with.

```
                                I
                            K  K  R
                         D  E  O  M  W
                      P  G  T  F  Q  J  V
                   Y  Y  Z  Q  D  M  B  L  P
                N  F  R  I  E  N  D  S  H  I  P
             J  J  M  J  G  N  U  S  R  D  F  Z  V
          Y  W  F  R  U  U  C  K  I  E  E  J  V  W  K
       O  X  S  X  G  N  I  Y  R  C  I  S  H  X  C  N  Z
    K  A  E  E  C  C  U  H  Q  Y  C  T  V  J  T  U  Z  M  N
 H  P  B  B  T  H  K  S  T  E  R  C  E  S  V  B  E  Y  K  U  Y
 N  R  F  X  V  L  Z  R  K  F  C  Z  S  P  R  M  G  N  G  X  F  F  E
M  N  G  U  I  G  A  V  F  R  F  N  K  F  M  B  U  O  F  G  O  D  F  K  E
B  I  S  D  C  A  R  C  A  J  G  T  H  G  A  T  E  M  I  C  U  X  T  K  T  X  B
M  R  R  W  B  U  V  G  M  M  E  F  G  T  S  N  U  R  D  D  S  M  R  Z  I  X  N  C  F
    D  A  M  I              N  E  M  P  A              A  Q  S  F
    V  G  L  I              D  X  F  H  X              Q  T  B  X
    Z  Y  I  B              F  Q  U  I  O              I  O  E  I
    J  U  H  Y              B  E  K  Z  L              R  M  L  M
    I  I  T  U              S  N  R  J  J              O  M  H  F
    U  P  W  D  Q  S  G  X  H  H  N  S  R  G  B  I  T  Y  J  R  H
    V  R  R  D  S  N  S  G  N  I  H  G  U  A  L  I  W  S  K  K  F
    T  N  N  K  I  M  L  E  R  I  J  Z  M  V  O  L  F  M  E  K  Y
    Y  U  A  R  B  B  K  W  N  X  M  U  S  N  Y  I  F  W  Q  F  H
    D  Y  A  O           E  E  S  I  I  T  N  Y  V  J  R  H  Q
    U  H  V  Z           Z  Y  S  I  Y  Q  Y  N  O  K  C  C  H
    S  L  H  P           P  P  J  O  J  V              S  N  O
    V  Q  B  Y           U  Q  K  R  L  Z              S  Y  I
    G  Q  V  V           X  S  N  V  U  C              E  M  G
    U  T  I  Z  F  A  G  W  R  I  X  Q  A  L           N  O  R
    I  K  L  C  W  Z  Y  T  I  N  U  H  D  O        B  I  Q  C
    L  S  X  L  T  L  E  M  A  R  K  Q  K  W           P  I  D
    J  K  T  W  U  P  S  T  Z  I  E  D  W  J           P  Y  K
    G  W  Z  S  J  F  P  Y  I  J  H  Q  F  F           A  Y  O
    R  H  I  E  S  X  W  N  Q  X  A  N  S  T           H  X  R
```

Find these words

CLOSENESS	FULL	LIFE
CRYING	FUN	SECRETS
EMOTION	HAPPINESS	SHARING
FAMILY	HARMONY	TOGETHER
FRIENDSHIP	LAUGHING	UNITY

Dot Square Game—Play with a friend!

Connect two flowers with a line. Take turns connecting flowers.
If you draw a line that completes a box, put your initials in that box—
it's yours! Whenever a player makes a box, they get to take another
turn. At the end of the game, count the boxes with your initials in it.
The player with the most boxes wins!

Use Your Head

*Trust in the L*ORD *with all your heart*
And do not lean on your own understanding.
PROVERBS 3:5 NASB

Swimming around in the icy Artic Ocean is an animal that's big, bulky, and weighs over 2,000 pounds. Beside it's long tusks, which can grow up to 3 ft. long, one of the most unique things about it is its head. If ice starts to form on the top of the ocean, the walrus's tiny but powerful head can hammer a hole through the ice. Talk about using your head.

Using your head isn't such a bad idea, not to pound a hole of course, but to solve a problem. Sometimes the answer you're praying for is just a matter of good sense. What is it that makes the most sense? While using common sense or your own understanding is a great idea, depending on that isn't. Check it out with a few others—your mom, your grandpa, someone you admire. Most importantly, go to God and ask him what he thinks.

When has your good common sense been an answer to prayer? Have you ever "leaned" on it and gotten into trouble?

Dear God, thanks for giving me common sense to make
decisions every day. Help me to listen to that sense and not
to ignore it. But I don't ever want to depend on just that.
Teach me to go to you first.

Choose a word for each part of speech specified.
Then use your words to fill in the story below.

1. _____ adjective

2. _____ verb

3. _____ noun

4. _____ verb (past tense)

5. _____ verb (past tense)

6. _____ verb (past tense)

7. _____ adjective

8. _____ verb

9. _____ noun

10. _____ verb

11. _____ place

12. _____ name

13. _____ adverb

14. _____ adjective

15. _____ verb (past tense)

16. _____ noun (plural)

17. _____ adverb

18. _____ verb

19. _____ number

20. _____ noun

21. _____ noun

22. _____ verb (past tense)

That Makes Sense!

I had a __1__ problem. I couldn't __2__ the __3__.

I __4__ my friends, and they __5__. We __6__,
and decided on the __7__ thing to do.

Our solution was to __8__ the __9__, and __10__ the __11__.

__12__ __13__ looked up how to get there.
It seemed __14__. We __15__ our __16__ and __17__ __18__.
After __19__ hours, we found __20__!

Now, my __21__ is fixed, and my problem is __22__.

The Big Picture

We know that God causes all things to work together
for good to those who love God, to those who are called
according to His purpose.

ROMANS 8:28 NASB

Village women in northern Thailand grow banana trees, rice,
melons, and sugar cane to help support their families. They also
weave beautiful patterns that start small and then grow into large
stretches of cloth used for scarves, bags, and clothes. Their hand
looms pull in different colored threads to create designs like blue
and white stripes or purple with tiny white dots.

God uses everything that happens to weave a beautiful design: the
ups and the downs and the days that are somewhere in between.
He's taking everything, both good and bad, to create an amazing
design. That design stretches beyond what happened Tuesday to
everything in your life, your school, your country, and across the
world. The pattern includes what's happened in history and what
will happen in the future.

You just see a little piece of the design and it doesn't always
make sense. When Jesus comes back and the pattern is finished,
everything will make sense.

Has something ever happened to you that didn't make sense?

Dear God, thank you that you're taking everything good and
everything bad in my life and in the world and working it
out for good. Even when I can't figure out what the pattern is,
you have the big picture in mind. I trust you.

Recreate the picture above in the grid below.

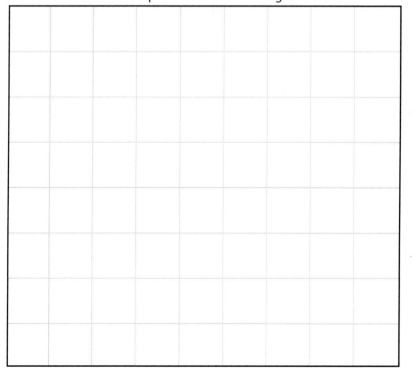

Horse Sense

It was a perfect summer day for a horseback ride. AJ put her foot
in the stirrup, swung a leg over the saddle and flipped the reins to
nudge Silver forward. "Come on, boy," she urged. "We're going for a
ride." The path ran through the forest, over a stone arch bridge, to
a large shimmering lake. *This is going to be great!* AJ thought.

Silver, though, had other ideas. He clip-clopped along as slowly
as he could. When AJ tugged the reins to go left, he went left but
circled around right. At this rate, they wouldn't ever reach the lake!

Sometimes we have our own ideas about what we should do, about
what's right and wrong. And we question God's path because
we don't feel like doing what he says, it doesn't make sense, or
everyone else is doing something different. But doing that means
missing out on not just what's good, but what's great. "I will guide
you on the *best* pathway for your life," he says. Don't settle for
second best.

*Dear God, I want what's best. Not just some of the time but
always. You're so faithful to lead. I'll be faithful to follow.*

Across the World

Ever since the world was created, people have seen the earth and sky. Through everything God made, they can clearly see his invisible qualities—his eternal power and divine nature. So they have no excuse for not knowing God.

ROMANS 1:20 NLT

In India a little girl giggles as she and her friends walk home from school for a lunch of *dahl*, or lentils, and rice. In Vietnam, a teenaged girl uses a sharp scythe to harvest rice and takes a break to wipe her forehead. In the USA, a sixth grade girl swings and hits a softball just beyond short stop and dashes for first base.

Three very different countries. Three very different girls. But wherever they are in the world, they can look up and see the same big sky and the same brilliant sun or moon.

That sun and moon shows God's power. The sky shows that he really is God. They're proof that he is God. No one can say, "But I didn't get a chance to see what you've done!" Everyone, everywhere has the privilege of seeing that God is good. It's as if God says, "Look up and see all that I've made, and you'll know that I am God."

Dear God, you are great! The other gods of the nations are just idols. They can't speak or hear or answer. But you made the heavens! Thanks for showing everyone everywhere how powerful you are.

Find your way
to the smile!

Start here

Star Light, Star Bright

*The heavens were made by the word of the LORD,
and all the stars, by the breath of His mouth.*

PSALM 33:6 HCSB

Look up at the sky on a clear summer night and you might see a white strip of very faint stars. That galaxy, called the Milky Way, has over 100 billion stars. The earth's bright fiery sun is just one of them.

Imagine a God so powerful that he made those billions of stars with a simple word. He spoke—and they came to be. He said, "Let there be light" and they appeared. He breathed and life was created. Imagine a God so powerful that he counts the stars in our galaxy and beyond. He keeps track of each one and calls them by name.

It's awesome and mind-blowing! That's the kind of God you serve. There's nothing he can't do: turn a tough situation upside down, change someone's heart, change your heart, provide what you need. He's an amazing God!

Dear God, you stretch out the heavens like a curtain. You sit above the circle of the whole earth. You are an amazing God! Thank you that there's nothing you can't do. Amen (Based on Isaiah 40:22).

```
                              G
                              N
                        J  I  D
                        L  Z  Z
                        Q  A  L
                  S  X  M  D  R
                  N  U  A  A  G
                  O  V  D  D  N
            M  I  T  A  I  I  H
            W  L  V  G  A  W  F
            W  L  T  Y  L  O  P
A  E  L  N  E  R  W  Q  A  N  G  F  I  Q  U  G  L  V  Z  I  W  A  Z  L  M  B  B  F  G
   A  A  M  I  L  K  Y  W  A  Y  O  B  B  A  Y  B  G  N  J  S  J  P  P  M  R  X  I
   M  K  B  B  J  M  U  D  D  P  L  G  U  D  X  A  O  C  P  S  V  I  X
   M  E  M  O  S  E  W  A  A  D  S  F  N  W  E  I  O  N  R  G  Y
      E  R  A  E  Q  X  T  U  M  Y  I  K  B  O  E  M  H  N
         G  R  R  Y  T  N  S  B  L  M  Q  B  V  G  T
         J  G  J  J  G  L  I  I  K  Y  A  U  L
            X  T  X  U  G  F  H  R  E  I  P
            A  A  L  H  V  X  A  H  H  M  P
            W  D  T  L  F  V  U  E  L  Z  U
         L  S  C  R  E  A  T  E  D  Z  P  T  Y
         N  E  S  R  E  V  I  N  U  A  R  B  M
         J  V  P  A  T  D        R  R  B  S  S  T
      A  E  J  O  O  N              W  A  Q  A  E  X
      I  W  X  E  O                 R  T  Q  F  C
      I  O  A                       S  Y  K
   D  C  R                          I  H  O
   L  T                             J  M
   H                                Z
```

Find these words

AMAZING	EARTH	MIND BLOWING
AWESOME	GALAXY	MOON
BILLIONS	HEAVENS	STAR
BRIGHT	LIGHT	SUN
CREATED	MILKY WAY	UNIVERSE

Beyond Talk

All hard work brings a profit,
but mere talk leads only to poverty.
PROVERBS 14:23 NIV

Jenna pulled out a pan of freshly baked cookies from the oven and set them on top of the stove.

"I wish I could bake," said Monica as she bit into a warm chocolate chip cookie and licked chocolatey goodness off her fingers.

"You could learn. I could teach you how to make my famous peanut butter and fudge cookies," Jenna said as she scooped cookie dough balls onto another cookie sheet.

"Well... I don't know. I'll think about."

You can wish or talk all you want or you can just do it. What have you always wanted to learn to do? Bake cupcakes, play piano, waterski, do a cartwheel, speak French? Go for it! Move past wishing and dreaming and make it happen.

Write down your goal. What do you want to achieve?

Write down the steps you'll need to take to make that goal happen.

Assess your commitment. How badly do you really want to reach your goal?

Ask someone to hold you accountable.

Write a plan and put it into action!

Dear God, I have so many "wants" swirling around in my head.
Instead of sitting around talking and dreaming,
give me the courage to take a chance and do!

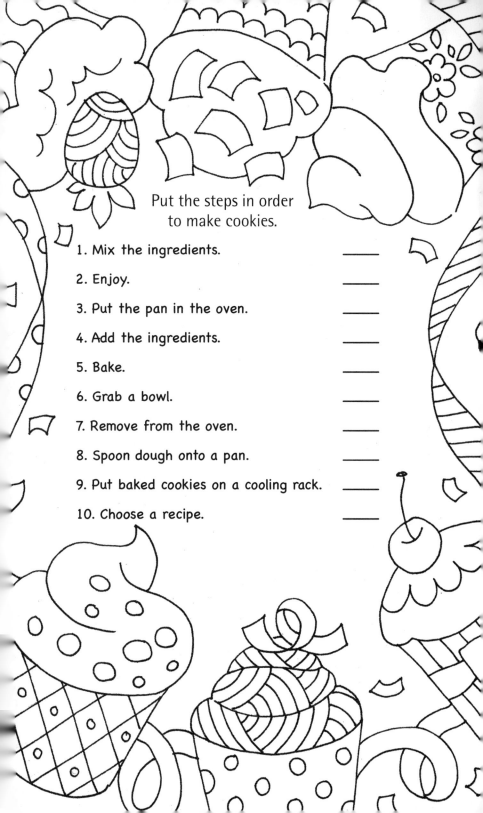

Put the steps in order
to make cookies.

1. Mix the ingredients.   ____

2. Enjoy.   ____

3. Put the pan in the oven.   ____

4. Add the ingredients.   ____

5. Bake.   ____

6. Grab a bowl.   ____

7. Remove from the oven.   ____

8. Spoon dough onto a pan.   ____

9. Put baked cookies on a cooling rack.   ____

10. Choose a recipe.   ____

Dot Square Game—Play with a friend!

Connect two flowers with a line. Take turns connecting flowers.
If you draw a line that completes a box, put your initials in that box—
it's yours! Whenever a player makes a box, they get to take another
turn. At the end of the game, count the boxes with your initials in it.
The player with the most boxes wins!

Pool Party Bust

*Be full of joy in the Lord always. I have learned to be satisfied
with the things I have and with everything that happens.*
PHILIPPIANS 4:4, 11 NCV

Ruined. Totally ruined. Jada watched rain pour down from the sky.
Tears streaked down her face. She felt miserable. Her pool party
birthday was a bust. All the cute beach decorations and party
favors wouldn't work for anything else.

There's nothing so disappointing as making plans and then having
them ruined. It's like everything you hoped for and worked for was
for nothing! What are you going to do?

- Option 1: Throw yourself on the bed and cry.

- Option 2: Call up your friend and tell them how miserable
  you are.

- Option 3: Call a couple of friends and ask for help finding a
  creative solution. Take on the challenge: How fast can you
  come up with a plan b that's better than plan a?

Being full of joy isn't easy, much less being content with the way
things turn out. Choosing to be thankful can turn a sour attitude
into a positive one. Finding a creative alternative might just turn a
flop into an unexpected surprise.

Have your plans ever flopped? What did you do?

*Dear God, I have been disappointed. I really wanted
one thing to happen, but something else did instead.
Help me to be content no matter what.*

Change one letter
to create new words and turn a
SOUR ATTITUDE into a GOOD ONE!

SOUR

_ _ _ _   Transfer liquid into a cup

_ _ _ _   Sulk

_ _ _ _   Place for ships to dock

_ _ _ _   Hiding place built with blankets

_ _ _ _   12 inches

_ _ _ _   Something to eat

GOOD

Adventure

You will fill me with joy in your presence.
PSALM 16:11 NIV

One bright Texas morning, Macie took her horse Samson out for a gallop. They dodged mesquite bushes scattered across her ranch and then cut across the path that led to her aunt and uncle's ranch.

This is the best! Macie thought as she leaned forward in the saddle. She lightened up on the reins and Samson surged forward. A rush of air whipped through her hair and she felt on top of the world.

You're on an adventure every day, an adventure called life. God's packed it with freedom, exhilaration, and pure joy! Don't let all your to-dos quiet the excitement of discovering what's new every day. Explore and enjoy everything God has for you.

Dear God, I'm looking forward to my life adventure with you!
Fill me with your joy. Help me to find and embrace
the new opportunities you bring my way.

Find your way
to the middle
of the garden.

Start here

Standing Up

Who will stand up for me against those who do evil?
PSALM 94:16 HCSB

Have you ever faced a dilemma that kept you up at night and turned your stomach into knots? That's exactly how Queen Esther felt. She was staring a problem in the face. Not just a little, it'll-go-away-in-a-few days problem; but a huge problem. Her people and her family were in danger. She had to ask the king for help.

If she *didn't* ask for help, her people were in trouble. If she *did* ask for help, *she* could be in trouble. No one, absolutely no one, went into the king's throne room without being called. Not even the queen. The punishment? Well, let's not go there.

Three days later Queen Esther walked into the throne room, not knowing what would happen. She just knew that she had to stand up.

God gave Queen Esther courage to do what she did. God gives you courage to stand up for what's right too. Courage to love someone who doesn't particularly like you. Courage to stand up for someone who can't speak up for herself. Courage to speak the truth even when it's not popular.

What is God asking you to be courageous about?

*Dear God, I'm not normally a courageous person.
Please take away my fear. If there's a deeper reason why I'm
afraid, show me what it is. Help me to stand up for what's right.*

1. Bright or daring

3. Honorably brave

5. Fact

6. Excellent moral character

DOWN

1. Confident in the face of fear

2. Truthfulness

4. Powerful

Complete the crossword puzzle with characteristics of people who stand up for what is right.

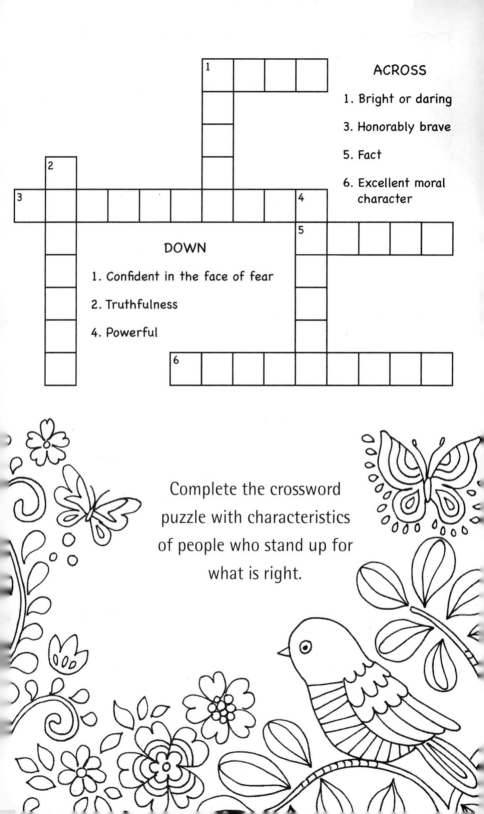

Splashes of Joy

The whole earth is filled with awe at your wonders;
where morning dawns, where evening fades,
you call forth songs of joy.
PSALM 65:8 NIV

Paisley stared outside her bedroom window at the rain. Rain had been coming down in buckets all day. The sun was nowhere to be seen and the skies were a dingy gray. Leaves and branches were drooping from the weight of constant rain. The small pond outside had been churned to a murky brown. *Not exactly the kind of day for a campout,* Paisley thought.

Ever had one of those days? A day when everything looks gloomy and nothing seems to turn out. You might be tempted to complain but what about going outside and catching raindrops with your tongue, or pulling on boots and jumping in a puddle (who says little kids get to have all the fun?), or cozying up inside with a book, or camping inside with blankets and pillows.

A day is what you make it. You can't always control what happens, but you can find the gift inside each day. Embrace your day!

Dear God, thank you for this day. I choose to wrap
my arms around it and enjoy it as a gift.
Help me discover new joys along the way.

Use the word **SPLASH** to create 20 new words.

S _ _ _ _   L _ _ _   S _ _ _   L _ _

S _ _ _ _   P _ _ _   S _ _ _   P _ _

A _ _ _   P _ _ _   A _ _   P _ _

L _ _ _   S _ _ _   A _ _   S _ _

L _ _ _   S _ _ _   H _ _   S _ _

Surprise

My child, listen and accept what I say.
Then you will have a long life. I am guiding you in the way
of wisdom, and I am leading you on the right path.
PROVERBS 4:10-12 NCV

Avery remembered the day like it was yesterday. Her dad had walked in the kitchen, sat down at the table, and said, "Avery, I want you to pack a bag tonight. You and I are going on a short trip tomorrow." She should have been excited but she really didn't want to miss hanging out with her friends that weekend.

"Where are we going? What are we going to do?" she asked.

All her dad said was, "You're going to need a swimsuit."

The next morning they drove north to a summer cabin. For the whole weekend, they swam and went tubing and skiing. Best of all, Avery got to be with her dad for three whole days. She closed her eyes and smiled. She loved remembering that day.

You won't always know what God has in mind when he tells you what to do. Sometimes he asks you to take the first step even if you don't understand, even if it doesn't make sense, even if you'd rather do something else.

What you can be sure of is this: God will lead you on the right path and it'll be good. God is full of surprises and his surprises are the best.

Dear God, I like to plan ahead and know what's coming next.
Thank you for being a God of surprises.
I trust you to do what's best.

Use the key below to figure out the secret message.

1	2	3	4	5	6	7	8	9	10	11	12	13
A	B	C	D	E	F	G	H	I	J	K	L	M

14	15	16	17	18	19	20	21	22	23	24	25	26
N	O	P	Q	R	S	T	U	V	W	X	Y	Z

___ ___ ___ ___ ___   ___ ___ ___ ___
4+1 2+20 2+3 6x3 5x5   4+3 5x3 10+5 2x2

___ ___ ___   ___ ___ ___ ___ ___ ___ ___
1x1 7x2 3+1   4x4 2+3 9x2 2x3 1+4 2+1 10x2

___ ___ ___ ___   ___ ___   ___ ___ ___ ___
3+4 3x3 3+3 4x5   4+5 10+9   2x3 3x6 3x5 10+3

___ ___ ___ ___ ___.   ___ ___ ___ ___ ___ 1:17
1x1 2x1 11+4 20+2 5x1   5x2 1x1 9+4 5x1 13+6

The Funny Side

Splendor and majesty are before him;
strength and joy are in his dwelling place.
1 Chronicles 16:27 niv

What do you think: Does God have a sense of humor or not?

The word "joy" pops up all through the Bible. Joy is in God's presence. God's Spirit gives joy. God's joy is our strength (Psalm 16:11; Galatians 5:22; Nehemiah 8:10). Joy is everywhere God is. With that joy comes laughter and a good dose of humor.

He made an elephant with a six-foot nose and family-pizza-size ears.

He made a giraffe with a neck as long as its legs.

He made tickle spots and funny bones and giggles and laughter.

Does God have a sense of humor?

Absolutely.

What's something that strikes you as funny?

Dear God, help me spot the creative, goofy, funny things
you've created and learn how to laugh.

Write down every second letter
to find the answer to the joke.

What is brown, hairy, and wears sunglasses?

Start
here

_ _ _ _ _ _ _ _

_ _ _ _ _ _ _ _ _ !

Dot Square Game—Play with a friend!

Connect two flowers with a line. Take turns connecting flowers.
If you draw a line that completes a box, put your initials in that box—
it's yours! Whenever a player makes a box, they get to take another
turn. At the end of the game, count the boxes with your initials in it.
The player with the most boxes wins!

Knitting

*I am certain that God, who began the good work within you,
will continue his work until it is finally finished on the day
when Christ Jesus returns.*

PHILIPPIANS 1:6 NLT

Click. Click.

"Hey, Ella. Whatcha doing?"

"Knitting a scarf for my fundraiser."

"A scarf?" said Harper looking at the small blue knit circle. "That doesn't look like a scarf. It looks more like a, well, like a coaster."

"Well, I'm not done yet. It'll be a scarf when I'm finished."

God isn't making a knit scarf, but he is making those who believe in Jesus into something beautiful. God has started a good work in you. You're not finished, but you're on the way. He's doesn't constantly compare you to perfection or point out your failures, and neither should you. He's still working to make you more and more like him.

What's true for you is true for others—God's not done with them yet. They're a work in progress. So while you may be tempted to complain or compare or criticize, don't. Encourage, believe in them, and pray for them instead. God is doing a good work—in them and in you!

*Dear God, thank you for loving me the way I am and
at the same time working to make me like you. Fill me with
hope that you're doing a good work in me and others.*

Use your creativity to design your own scarf!

Looking Behind

*I know your deeds, your love and faith,
your service and perseverance, and that you are
now doing more than you did at first.*
REVELATION 2:19 NIV

"Paddle harder, Madison!" her dad called above the wind and rain. Madison plunged her paddle into the water and pulled back hard. In the canoe next to her, Madison saw her brothers do the same. *Plunge, pull, and out.* Repeat. *Plunge, pull, and out.*

Their campsite was all the way across the mile-long lake. Even though they'd been paddling for half an hour, the opposite shore seemed far away. That was when Madison looked back and saw how far they'd actually come. All this hard paddling *was* paying off.

Working toward a goal is great. But when that goal is still a long ways off, looking back can be encouraging. It shows you how far you've come. Maybe you're science grade isn't up to an A, but you got an A on the last quiz. Maybe you can't do a cartwheel on the beam, but remember when you struggled to learn the split jump? Maybe you can't reach high E on your horn, but remember when you didn't know a quarter note from a half note? Look how far you've come!

On your way to moving forward, take a break and look back. See how far you've come!

Dear God, thanks for progress. On my way toward my goals, remind me to look back and appreciate how far I've come.

Start
here

Style with a Smile

Happiness makes a person smile.
PROVERBS 15:13 NCV

"Grace!" Grace's mom called from down the stairs. "Are you dressed yet? We're leaving for the wedding in ten minutes."

Grace looked at herself in the mirror. Party dress. *Check.* Matching shoes. *Check.* Matching purse. *Check.* Hair styled. *Check.*

"Coming, Mom!" Grace spun around, looked again in the mirror and put on the finishing touch—a big smile.

Whether you're in a swimsuit at the beach or suited up in your hockey gear, a smile is the finishing touch on whatever you put on. A smile makes you look good and feel good. It makes those around you feel good too. Wouldn't you rather hang out with someone smiling than someone who's always frowning?

A smile starts when you choose joy. That doesn't mean nothing bad ever happens or that you never feel sad. You look for the good things God gives. When you do, it'll show on your face!

Dear God, thank you for your joy that bubbles up inside me. Just thinking about all you do puts a smile on my face.

```
        S Y G L J O Y H          I P F Z E G V K
      B E I T L X Q X I I      O Q E S B L G U A J
      Y T V W Z Y W X I H E    L F F H U I D Q R S M
    P R     T I X O V C E A X E   F N S C X D L J F V     R D
  W S I C     J F T U T G E D S   E O W U P M F N A     S J M L
  G F G B Y X I T F X C P O Z   R T N O F L F P F M V P X M
  D E X R D H M P U G D P M C   H Q A T Y G Y N I F G I J D
  X L B D O S K F I O J W C A   E O H G G L M L K T E H I Y
  T S G N I L E E F Y M T M E   P F C N J D E F B A C A T H
  L T P X N Y F H E I W G T N   O B Q I P D G D X C U B V E
  B N U F A L J B R Y Z D F I G D G R H U U A K F S C G L X
  Q S F P F X Q R A R Y L R W Z C C S S X Z S F A S H I O N
    M K C E W O J V W Y Q R E P L G U I G N A S Q M T X W
      G A H R T N A S A E L P S J J H N X E E G C I K D
                Q N K Y H S W S I
      V N T A V E P G Q U S V Q C E C F V K K K A K O M
    A P N W L I T H C F S L Y L M W D I X C T B V D R C D
  G J U Z L J S R H C E L T S B X A A U Q N E C Y R A K O V
  R M N I H P K T D N Y S R L A F T T B P P O H C T D W R J
  R X C Q M C G N I S S E L B   J X E D H U W S H Q U U U S
  E A Z V B E I P R R P U W A   T N E M T N E T N O C A G B
  T D D T Q B P E Z H I B C A   Y V P D P K J V L H C C E J
  I C R T F A U W I A G C G S   E Y E Q F W J D W X O O C B
  K S Q R H J F O X Y O D P T   W I J A G X S E C I O H C X
  E N N Y   N R G N K Z D X Y   J N Q F C E L A Q   N Z B Z
    B H   O A D L W H T H U L   M X C L D F B P G S   Z Q
      L N J U T M A I H P E   L H N S K I S M X W H
      G D H U C A M D A P       N A I A D P Q K T L
      W O D G A C M Z           C E X C J D G I
```

Find these words

BEAUTY	FASHION	MIRROR
BLESSING	FEELINGS	OUTFIT
CHOICES	FINISHING TOUCH	PLEASANT
CONTENTMENT	HAPPINESS	SMILE
DRESSED UP	JOY	STYLE

When It's Dark Outside

"You are the light of the world—like a city on a hilltop that cannot be hidden. No one lights a lamp and then puts it under a basket. Instead, a lamp is placed on a stand, where it gives light to everyone in the house."
MATTHEW 5:14-15 NLT

Lights shine best in the darkness. Turn the light switch on in the middle of the day, and you'll hardly notice. But light a campfire against the backdrop of a midnight sky and you'll see that fire from miles around.

If you're living for Jesus, you're like a light to the world. Don't huddle around where there's a lot of light already. In other words, don't spend all your time with Christians and at church. Get to know people who don't realize how much God loves them.

- Write an I-hope-you're-having-a-great-day note to someone in your class.

- Offer to return someone's cart at the grocery store.

- Sign up for a sport with kids you don't know.

- Join an after-school club.

Then tell and show the people you meet about Jesus.

Dear Jesus, you are the light of the world. Because you live inside me, I can be the light to the world too. Show me different ways to spread your light to those who don't know you.

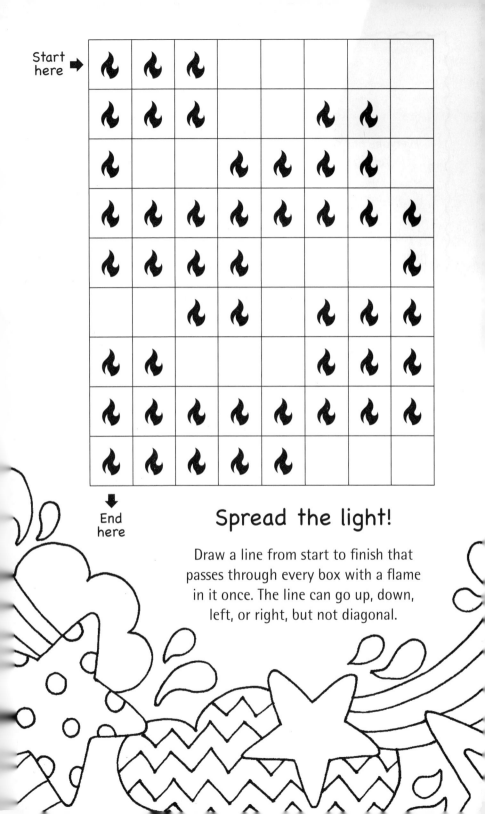

Start here →

End here ↓

Spread the light!

Draw a line from start to finish that passes through every box with a flame in it once. The line can go up, down, left, or right, but not diagonal.

What It Is

*Everyone has sinned; we all fall short of God's glorious standard.
Yet God, in his grace, freely makes us right in his sight.
He did this through Christ Jesus.*

ROMANS 3:23-24 NLT

If you look at any magazine cover, you'll see perfect-looking people. Shiny hair, straight teeth, flawless skin. Never mind that in real life they're no different from anyone else. You just don't notice because they've been altered digitally to cover up imperfections.

No one's perfect even though they'd like you to think they are. They're not perfect on the outside; they're not perfect on the inside. When it comes to perfection, only God is perfect. He's holy, perfect in love, kindness, and goodness. No one else is like him.

When you do what's wrong, your imperfection is showing. If you own up to that sin, God shares his perfection with you. He makes you right in his sight when you call sin what it is—wrong. And he doesn't just cover it up like they do in magazines. Through Jesus, he makes us completely right. Holy and acceptable.

When you call sin what it is, God gives grace!

*Dear God, I want to call it like it is. No pretending, disguising,
or ignoring. If there's something in my life that makes you sad
and keeps me from having the best relationship possible with you,
please show me what it is. So I can call it what it is and
ask for your forgiveness.*

Circle the two pictures that are exactly the same.

Pelicans

*Teach me your way, Lᴏʀᴅ, that I may rely on your faithfulness;
give me an undivided heart, that I may fear your name.*
PSALM 86:11 NIV

Louisiana is called the Pelican State. Across its coast, brown pelicans dive headfirst into the ocean and use their large pouch-like beaks to scoop up fresh fish for dinner.

Seagulls like fish too, though, and instead of catching their own, they sit on a pelican's head and distract it by pecking its head. *Peck, peck, peck.* That distraction can cost the pelican a tasty lunch if the seagull snatches the fish away.

Distractions can cost you too. Distracted during a class? It could mean missing directions important for a good grade. Distracted while a friend is talking about her very bad day? It could mean she gets upset and says you don't care. Distracted by your phone while doing homework? It could mean homework takes two hours instead of one.

The biggest distraction to avoid is when other things become more important than loving God with all your heart. Distractions might be tempting, but they take away a better reward.

Dear God, sometimes it's hard for me to focus because I don't feel like it or because something else seems more interesting. Teach me to give everything I've got to whatever I'm doing.

Figure out the secret message by using the code below.

◎	▲	☼	□	♦	✓	❖	◆	✿	✝	☺	✏	〰
A	B	C	D	E	F	G	H	I	J	K	L	M

★	↑	↓	●	⌘	⚙	✗	✳	回	✺	✂	※	❄
N	O	P	Q	R	S	T	U	V	W	X	Y	Z

〰※ ♦※♦⚙ ◎⌘♦ ✓✿✂♦□
↑★ ※↑✳, ⚙↑回♦⌘♦✿❖★ ✏↑⌘□,
✿★ ※↑✳ ✿ ✗◎☺♦ ⌘♦✓✳❖♦.
↓⚙◎✏〰 141:8

__ ____ ___ _____

__ ___, _____ ____,

__ ___ _ ____ _____.

_____ 141:8

Dot Square Game—Play with a friend!

Connect two flowers with a line. Take turns connecting flowers.
If you draw a line that completes a box, put your initials in that box—
it's yours! Whenever a player makes a box, they get to take another
turn. At the end of the game, count the boxes with your initials in it.
The player with the most boxes wins!

Praying Flowers

The heavens declare the glory of God;
the skies proclaim the work of his hands.
They have no speech, they use no words;
no sound is heard from them.
Yet their voice goes out into all the earth,
their words to the ends of the world.
PSALM 19:1, 3-4 NIV

If you hiked through the desert you probably wouldn't come across a talking cactus or praying flowers. If you walked through the jungle, you wouldn't come across trees that preach.

The sun doesn't sing, the moon doesn't journal, and the stars don't shout, "Hallelujah!" But they still manage to praise God—not with words, but through their beauty. Without a word or sound, the stars and sky talk about God's glory and say, "God is amazing!"

Pink roses and prickly cactus praise him.

Smelly skunks and mooing cows praise him.

Streaking comets and lightning strikes praise him.

Everything in all creation praises him.

What in creation just makes you want to praise him?

Dear God, your creation is amazing! I love seeing and hearing your wonderful works. They praise you and I want to praise you too!

Unscramble the words to reveal the names
of some popular flowers.

IROHCD _ _ _ _ _ _

SDYAI _ _ _ _ _

RFWUELSNO _ _ _ _ _ _ _ _ _

SORE _ _ _ _

PILUT _ _ _ _ _

YLLI _ _ _ _

OTACNIRAN _ _ _ _ _ _ _ _ _

FIOLADDF _ _ _ _ _ _ _ _

UEANPTI _ _ _ _ _ _ _

ETIVOL _ _ _ _ _ _